14.95

W9-DEG-223   9604

x595.789 Hunt.J

Hunt, Joni Phelps, 1956-

A shimmer of butterflies

c1995.

JUN 2 4 1996

CLOSE-UP
A Focus on Nature

SILVER BURDETT PRESS
© 1995 Silver Burdett Press
Published by Silver Burdett Press.
A Simon & Schuster Company
299 Jefferson Road, Parsippany, NJ 07054
Printed in the United States of America
10 9 8 7 6 5 4 3 2 1

All rights reserved including the right of
reproduction in whole or in part in any form.

Library of Congress
Cataloging-in-Publication Data
Hunt, Joni Phelps, 1956-
Butterflies: monarchs, moths & more--up
close & unexpected/by Joni Phelps Hunt; pho-
tographs by Stanley Breeden . . . [et al.].
p. cm. -- (Close up)
ISBN 0-382-24874-0 (LSB)
ISBN 0-382-24875-9 (SC)
1. Butterflies--Juvenile literature. 2. Moths--
Juvenile literature. [1. Butterflies. 2. Moths.]
I. Breeden, Stanley, 1937 or 8- ill. II. Title.
III. Series: Close up (Parsippany, N.J.)
QL544.2.H86 1994
595.78'9--dc20   94-30872
                                         CIP
                                         AC

FANFARE: *Hairy spines on the archduke caterpillar help to scare off hungry birds.*

A SHIMMER OF

Butterflies

WRITER
Joni Phelps Hunt

SERIES EDITOR
Vicki León

PHOTOGRAPHERS
*Stanley Breeden, D. Cavagnaro, Hal Clason, Michael Fogden,
Jeff Foott, John Gerlach, Richard R. Hansen, Martha Hill, Alex Kerstitch,
Frans Lanting, Robert and Linda Mitchell, Jeanette Sainz, Kjell B. Sandved,
Kevin Schafer, Larry Ulrich, Larry West, Belinda Wright*

DESIGNER
Ashala Nicols Lawler

SILVER BURDETT PRESS
© 1995 Silver Burdett Press
Published by Silver Burdett Press.
A Simon & Schuster Company
299 Jefferson Road,
Parsippany, NJ 07054
Printed in the United States of America
10 9 8 7 6 5 4 3 2 1
All rights reserved including the right of reproduction in whole or in part in any form.

EVANSTON PUBLIC LIBRARY
CHILDREN'S DEPARTMENT
1703 ORRINGTON AVENUE
EVANSTON, ILLINOIS 60201

Nature's sparkling gems

A SPLASH OF BRILLIANCE. A SHEEN, a shimmer of beauty flutters by. I glimpse a butterfly in flight and my heart soars with it. Before its astonishing transformation this creature crept along as a caterpillar. I'm in awe of such a metamorphosis. I consider the implications. Do we all have within us this potential to grow and change?

Butterflies and moths grace nearly all the earth and have done so for millions of years. They're masters of disguise and shameless copycats, simply to survive. Some travel thousands of miles in mass migrations. Others spend their life cycles on an acre or two. Lest you think they get by on looks alone, be assured they earn their place in the natural world as pollinators.

Inevitably, these insects suffer as the health of the environment declines. Loss of their natural habitat and pollution endanger butterflies and moths. Their loss robs precious jewels of inspiration from our lives.

WHAT ARE LEPIDOPTERA?

LIKE POINTS OF PIGMENT in an Impressionist painting, millions of tiny scales combine their colors to create just one butterfly wing. The Greek words Lepis (scale) and pteron (wing) together form the scientific name for butterflies and moths – Lepidoptera. This kind of insect differs from all others by the colorful scales on its wings and a hollow tongue that uncoils to sip food.

Scientists who study moths and butterflies, called lepidopterists, can identify more than 165,000 species. Butterflies account for nearly 20,000 species, and moths make up the rest. Only one kind of insect, the beetle, has more species than Lepidoptera. They're not the oldest insects, but fossil evidence shows that butterflies and moths have lived on earth at least 130 million years.

During their long stay, these winged creatures have settled everywhere except the polar caps and icy mountains. Butterflies and moths live in woodlands, meadows, and tropical rainforests. Their other homes include arctic tundra, high mountain ranges, islands, deserts, ponds, and swamps.

As the world's smallest butterfly, the pygmy blue has a wingspan of less than one-half inch. It lives in both California desert mountains at altitudes of 6,000 feet and Death Valley at 178 feet below sea level. Papua New Guinea is home to the largest butterfly, the nearly 12-inch Queen Alexandra birdwing. The atlas moth of Asia with its one-foot wingspan is thought to be the world's largest flying insect.

TAPESTRY IN MOTION
Butterfly wings rival Persian carpets in color and pattern. Some of the largest wings belong to the Australian Cairns birdwing butterfly, left, and wing detail, below. Demand for birdwings by collectors prompted Australia to protect them. Above, a butterfly sips nectar through its strawlike tongue.

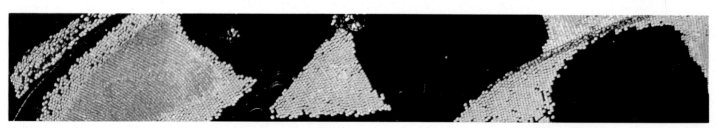

WINGED WONDERS

THE BODIES OF BUTTERFLIES AND MOTHS HAVE three parts: head, thorax, and abdomen. The entire body is covered in flat hairs; the wings have short, scalelike hair. The head contains antennas, eyes, and a mouth or tongue. The two antennas act as sensors for smell and touch. Made up of between seven and 100 small segments, a butterfly's antennas are usually thin with a small knob on the end. Those of a moth end in a point or can look like feathers.

Large eyes located on the sides of the head perceive shapes, colors, patterns, and movements nearby. The eyes have no long-distance vision, as do birds and mammals. Instead they recognize a compound image, made up of thousands of smaller images. Unlike a human eye, a compound eye cannot move or keep an object in focus as it comes close.

The eyes of some butterflies and many moths can see what human eyes cannot. They see ultraviolet light reflected or absorbed by patterns on flowers and on other butterflies. This helps them locate food and potential mates in their own species.

The nickname "four eyes" aptly describes species with an extra pair of eyes. Called simple eyes, they're set above the compound eyes and are partly covered by scales. Simple eyes cannot form an image, but they are sensitive to light and influence how the compound eyes see.

Since butterflies have been on earth so long, it's not surprising that parts of them would change over time. They originally had mouth parts that could chew. As more flowering plants appeared on earth, the mouths of most species changed to a tongue. Called a proboscis, the hollow tongue is used like a straw. It stays curled close beneath the front of the head until the insect uncoils it to drink.

The thorax or midsection anchors four wings and three pairs of legs. At least four, and sometimes all six, legs are strong and have hooks at the tips to grasp a perch. Along with the mouth and antennas, the soles of the feet may contain taste buds. For these species, alighting on flowers with even a trace of sweetness triggers the tongue to roll out like a party favor.

BUTTERFLY OR MOTH?

Exceptions aside, butterflies fly by day, have knobs at antennas' end, hold wings above the body at rest, and form a chrysalis. Moths generally fly at night, have pointed, sometimes feathery antennas, stretch wings flat upon landing, spin a cocoon, and have stout, furry bodies. The butterfly above has a compound eye and pollen coating the coiled tongue.

A male atlas moth, right, flashes extra-sensory antennas.

A butterfly's wings – miniature marvels of aerodynamics – lift it to soar through the sky. A medium-sized butterfly's body weighs about the same as a large bee, but its wings are about 20 times larger than the bee's. Front wings carry the creature in flight, and without them there is no liftoff. Back wings help glide, change speed, and steer. They may be torn or broken, but that won't ground the flight.

Wing scales overlap like shingles laid on a roof to create abundant colors and patterns. Each lightweight scale is a hardened cell attached to the wing by a stalk. Scales add strength to the wings and aid flight. Even gently rubbing a wing will remove thousands of scales or powdery butterfly dust.

What gives wings their rich, often radiant colors? Either pigment or the wing structure. Similar to clothing dyes, pigments color scales in black, gray, brown, yellow, orange, and red.

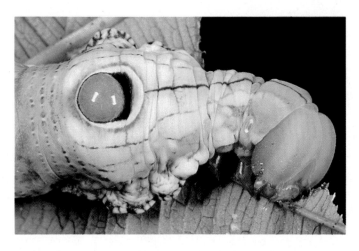

Iridescent greens, and vivid blues and violets result from the way a wing is made. Light hitting the layers of a wing creates vibrant color, similar to sunlight shining through a crystal.

The wings of blue morpho butterflies found in the American tropics reflect light and produce one of nature's most dazzling colors. A typical morpho in Brazil has 15 square inches of wing surface. On each square inch are 165 rows of scales, with

LET'S FACE IT...
Caterpillars come in all sizes, shapes, and colors. The Costa Rican butterfly larva, far left, swells in a snake pose to scare off predators. White eggs on its face were laid by a parasitic fly. An Australian gum emperor moth caterpillar, above, uses red mouth parts to grasp food. A large false eye on its back helps protect the Malaysian cyclops hawk moth caterpillar, left.

FLOWER POWER BROKER

*H*igh-energy pollinators, swallow-tail butterflies have distinctive tails at wings' end. Their strong legs clutch flowers and their wings flutter while probing for nectar. A western tiger swallowtail, left, sips from a thistle.

600 scales in each row, totaling 99,000 scales. The wings of a single morpho hold nearly 1.5 million scales.

A few butterflies have transparent wings. Known as glasswing butterflies, only their delicate veins show. Some found in Central and South American jungles become almost invisible when landing on the forest floor.

The final body section of butterflies and moths, the abdomen, is covered by scales and hairs. It carries the digestive system, and reproductive and scent organs.

FIRST UP – THE BUTTERFLY OR THE EGG?

FAMILY TIES

Bright pastel palm king butterfly eggs, below, preview the markings of adults to come. At right, you're seeing double as two pairs of this Malaysian rainforest species mate.

WHAT MAY SEEM LIKE A BUTTERFLY'S carefree, random flight actually has urgency. An adult butterfly's entire life can be as short as one week or as long as eight to ten months, depending on its species. The typical life span covers only two weeks. Its erratic flight path helps keep birds from catching it and allows it to find a mate and produce offspring quickly.

The male butterfly takes a long flight to look for a mate. Some also have scales or hairy fringe that scatter a scent to attract females. With moths, it's the female that releases scent from glands in the abdomen. A male moth's feathery antennas identify the perfume – as far as several miles away – and track it to the source. With swallowtail butterflies, where females of one species may impersonate another for protection, the female chooses a mate to eliminate problems of mistaken identity.

During her lifetime a female butterfly may lay several dozen tiny eggs or as many as 1500. She often flies many miles to find just the right place to leave them. Using sensors on her feet and antennas, she chooses specific plants to serve as food after the eggs hatch into caterpillars.

The female lays eggs on the underside of leaves, stems, or flowers. There the eggs are shaded from sun, rain, and hungry predators. A fluid released with the eggs helps glue them in place and may protect them from drying out.

Although moths also give their eggs protective cover, they choose from a wider variety of host plants. The fritillary butterfly drops its eggs randomly while flying. After hatching, fritillary caterpillars search for food that suits them.

The type of eggs laid varies by species. Eggs can be laid in a large group, in small clusters, or singly. One European moth lays eggs in a ring around a twig. Eggs can be round or shaped like a cone, dome, spindle, or turban. Many have patterned ridges. Most newly laid eggs appear as pale white, yellow, or green. As they develop, the eggs darken, often taking on patterns and colors of the soon-to-be caterpillar.

An egg can hatch in as little as two days or as long as one year. The usual time is five to seven days. The new caterpillar chews a hole, wriggles out and eats the egg shell, which contains nutrients for its growth.

THE EXTREMELY HUNGRY CATERPILLAR

T HE TINY CATERPILLAR OR LARVA begins to eat plant leaves. And eat. And eat. In about a day's time it gobbles twice its weight in food. The caterpillar eats so much food, it grows to nearly 1,000 times its original weight.

How does its body expand while it grows so much? When stretched to the limit, a caterpillar's outer covering, called an exoskeleton, splits behind its head. The caterpillar stops eating, spins a silk pad to anchor its legs, and begins shrugging off its cover. This process, known as molting, usually happens four or five times. The caterpillar nearly doubles in size every time it molts.

ON THE WING
A male Japanese kite butterfly hovers over the female in a courtship dance. Not long after an adult begins to fly, a short courtship begins, with chases, dances, and caresses.

Caterpillars bear no resemblance to the creatures they will become. The head has a pair of simple eyes, short antennas, and strong jaws with sharp cutting edges to devour plants. The thorax has three sections, the abdomen ten.

No trace of future wings shows on an earthbound caterpillar. Instead, eight pairs of legs help it ripple along. The first three pairs grasp leaves or other food while feeding. The other ten legs have stiff hooks on the end called crotchets. As the flat end of each foot contacts a smooth surface, the center draws up, creating a suction-cup effect. The caterpillar contracts muscles just below the outer surface to move along in a wavelike motion.

Caterpillars come in as many colors and shapes as butterflies and moths do. This variety helps camouflage them from predators like birds, frogs, lizards, wasps, ants, and small mammals. To keep enemies guessing, their outsides after molting may look far different than earlier coverings.

Among disguises they use are markings that look like a snake, a dead leaf, or bird droppings. A caterpillar might have two whiplike tails, horns, or sharp – sometimes poisonous – spines. Another might have long hairs growing out of its body to discourage birds from snapping up a caterpillar canapé. Dense hairs on the caterpillar of the woolly bear moth can cause allergic reactions. A furry coat also keeps small insects from laying parasitic eggs.

Caterpillars feeding on poisonous plants hold the toxins in their system. To warn predators of their foul and sometimes deadly taste, they're likely decorated with spots or stripes and wear bright pink, green, yellow, red, or orange.

Curious partnerships or symbiosis exist between some caterpillars and some ants.

METAMORPHOSIS – MUNCHER TO MONARCH

*A monarch butterfly caterpillar
munches milkweed, right,
storing fat for the coming change.
When ready to become a pupa,
the caterpillar hangs from a branch
with its tail curled up
like the letter "J."
As its outer cover becomes loose,
the exposed pupa squirms until
the covering begins to fall off,
middle right. Without its outer skin,
the pupa forms a hard casing
called a chrysalis, far right.
Chrysalis comes from a Greek word
meaning gold.*

In the mountainous forests near Veracruz, Mexico, a caterpillar from the metal mark butterfly family interacts with carpenter ants. While the caterpillar feeds at night on the croton plant, ants protect it from wasps and robber ants. In return, the carpenter ants lick drops of honeydew oozing from a gland on the caterpillar's back. During the day, ants coax the caterpillar off the croton into a small underground chamber they dig at the base of the plant. Sealed inside, it is protected from enemies and from grass fires set by native tribes.

In Europe and Asia, the caterpillar of some species of butterflies known as blues must rely on ants for survival. In return for the caterpillar's sugary nectar, the ants carry it into their nest. Because the caterpillar looks like the ant young and uses similar begging behavior, it is fed by adult ants. Without their help, it's likely the caterpillar would starve.

Some caterpillars, especially of moths, can destroy crops, forests, clothing, and grain. The greatest damage comes when a species is introduced to an area. Without its natural predators, the population soars. The Asian gypsy moth has decimated millions of acres of forest in Siberia and China. Its move to the west coast of the United States threatens conifer forests and valley oak forests.

PUPA –
BETWEEN EARTH & SKY

WHEN PREPARING FOR metamorphosis, the transformation to butterfly, a caterpillar spins a small pad of silk on a leaf or twig. A hook at the end of the caterpillar's abdomen grasps the pad before its outer covering splits and is shed one last time. The caterpillar is now a pupa encased in a chrysalis covering. It hangs freely suspended or supported by a silk thread around its middle. The word pupa comes from a Latin word meaning doll because its usual shape looks like a small doll wrapped in blankets.

The moth caterpillar forms a cocoon from silk glands in its mouth. Some spin a heavy coat of silk to cover the pupa. Others use only a light silk gauze cover. Several species of moth caterpillars dig a burrow as protection while a pupa.

The pupal stage usually lasts from two to three weeks. Or it may run from a few days to several years, depending on the species. During this time, hormones turn basic structures already within the caterpillar into butterfly parts. As it develops, the pupa's shape shows where wings, eyes, antennas, and often other body parts are located.

While a pupa, the insect can move only within its covering. To confuse predators, most are camouflaged by color and shape. The chrysalis can look like a twig, leaf, flower bud, rock, or dewdrop. It can even have spines or horns. Sealed in its casing, a pupa cannot feed either, so it uses fat reserves stored while a caterpillar. Air reaches the pupa through breathing holes called spiracles.

Suddenly the chrysalis moves, shakes. The sheath splits, signaling metamorphosis is complete. First a head emerges. Then thorax, legs, wings, and finally the abdomen. Its wings wrinkled and damp, the adult butterfly hangs on the broken chrysalis to let them dry. Flexing the wings pumps blood through the veins and causes them to expand. When the blood returns to the body, the hollow veins harden like struts to support the wing. After at least an hour and sometimes as long as a day, the butterfly can try out its wings.

FLIGHT SCHEDULES

 ERTAIN FLIGHT RESTRICTIONS come with a new pair of wings. Like a solar panel collecting the sun's energy, a butterfly must sunbathe until its internal temperature reaches about 65° Fahrenheit. Only then are the wing muscles strong enough for flight. Night-flying moths make up for lack of the sun's warmth by vibrating their wing muscles to generate enough heat for takeoff.

Climate affects a butterfly's movements. In temperate regions, a dew-covered butterfly on a chilly morning in spring is temporarily grounded. Mountain and coastal species wait until mist or fog lifts before flight. In late afternoon they find shelter for the night. During storms they find refuge under rocks or plants.

BREAKTHROUGH!
Inside the chrysalis a monarch pupa wiggles and changes. After at least a week, the outer sheath becomes clear, showing the new butterfly's true colors. The insect splits its covering and forces its way out head first, above. Wings crumpled and useless, the butterfly crawls onto the sheath, right. As fluid flows through the wings, they harden. In an hour or more, they'll be ready for flight.

MIRROR IMAGE

*M*alayan lacewing butterflies show their striking
underwings. Like the
wings of many species, one side is
showy, the other side drab.

In arctic areas butterflies travel no more than two feet above ground to make use of the sun's warming rays reflected off the earth. Desert species are active near dawn or dusk when the air is warm, but stay sheltered during the heat of the day.

Crowded skies in the tropics hold the largest number and variety of species. Moist heat allows butterflies to be on the wing from before dawn until after dusk. When not feeding near a stream or cleared area, they usually find their way to cooler woods and the tops of trees.

Since butterflies lose their ability to fly at about 40°F, they must hibernate during cold weather in many regions of the world. Different species have adapted to hibernate at different stages in the life cycle.

When fritillary butterfly eggs hatch in August and September, the new caterpillar goes directly into hibernation, without as much as a meal. Viceroy butterfly caterpillars grow until their third molt, then curl inside a leaf for winter protection. Full-grown swallowtail caterpillars extend the length of their stay as a pupa to last through winter. Even adult butterflies of some species seek out sheltered areas to hang with wings tightly closed until spring thaw begins.

With body systems nearly shut down during hibernation, the insect can tolerate cold of -20°F. A caterpillar snoozes in frozen ground or even in water. A pupa encased in a chrysalis or cocoon can be buried in deep snow drifts.

EGGSPECTING

After mating, the female searches for a plant to later serve as food for her caterpillars. A Costa Rican pierid butterfly, right, deposits yellow, spindle-shaped eggs. Smooth, round eggs, top right, are from a northern pearly eye butterfly in Michigan.

When the weather warms, their life cycle continues from where it was before the interruption.

While tropical butterflies don't hibernate, one lepidopterist has studied a group – the poisonous ithomiids of the American tropics – that follows a strict daily schedule. They feed from flowers beginning at 5:30 a.m. and finish three hours later as other species begin. When afternoon clouds darken the sky, ithomiids fly into rainforest clearings to sip nectar from white flowers easily visible in dim light. They save active pursuits for midday hours when the sun's rays furnish extra energy. New butterflies emerge between 9 and 10 a.m. Courtship and mating occur between 10 a.m. and 1 p.m. Finally, females search out suitable plants and lay eggs from 10:30 a.m. to 1:30 p.m.

FILING A FLIGHT PLAN

HOW FAST CAN A BUTTERFLY FLY? THOSE CALLED pierids and blues cruise at under five miles per hour (mph). The daggerwing of Costa Rica skims along at ten to 25 mph. The giant skipper of Mexico holds the speed record at 42 mph.

One of the most amazing feats in nature is the migration of millions of seemingly fragile butterflies over thousands of miles. More than 200 species throughout the world have been known to migrate. Some species move with the seasons. Overpopulation triggers other migrations when adults must find new food sources for offspring. Still others migrate when their habitat is destroyed.

The numbers of butterflies joining in migrations are difficult to fathom. In Ceylon, a migration of three species of sulphur butterflies was estimated at 26,000 butterflies per minute along a one-mile area. The Australian bogong moth travels in huge numbers from the north to caves in the southern alps. Along the way in resting areas, they cover walls of buildings and even stall factory machinery. In Africa, swarms of migrant butterflies crisscross the continent south of the Sahara. Cars often overheat after the radiators become clogged with dead butterflies.

The painted lady butterflies found in Asia, Europe, Africa, and America are champion migrators. In spring they fly north from Africa and the Middle East into Europe, even crossing the Alps. They venture into India, south along the west coast of Africa, and north to Iceland. In North America one generation leaves Mexico in spring, another arriving in Canada and Newfoundland in late summer. During one three-day migration an estimated three billion painted ladies flew across a 40-mile-wide area of California.

Another frequent flier, the orange-and-black monarch butterfly migrates from Canada south to milder temperatures each winter. The 3,000- to 4,000-mile trek begins each July for an estimated 100 million monarchs. They've been known to fly up to 100 miles a day and reach speeds of 30 mph, although typical flight speed is ten mph.

As many as five million monarchs from western Canada settle in ten sites each October, reaching south from Mendocino in California to Ensenada in Baja California. The rest, from central and eastern Canada, fly south to Florida, Mexico, Central America, and Cuba. Each site they choose has a source of fresh water and tall trees.

VANISHING ACT

Butterflies use camouflage to avoid predators. Shape, color, and pattern of the underwings help the autumn leaf butterfly, top, become just another leaf on the rainforest floor. Like the imperial moth from Iowa, lower left, many moths resemble plants or tree bark. This coloring lets them rest safely during daylight hours.

ALL THAT GLITTERS...

Tropical species come in many colors, and often can change hues. Light hitting curved wing scales reflects various shades on a South American blue morpho butterfly, far left. "Blue" scales seen through a microscope actually look brown or transparent. The day-flying sunset moth of Madagascar also has brilliant structural wing colors, above. The fringed tails help it fly without a sound.

Before leaving Canada, monarchs fill up on nectar and store fat to use as energy during winter when flowers with nectar are scarce. During cool temperatures at winter quarters, monarchs cluster together tightly on trees, each attached to a leaf by its gripper feet. They exist in a state of semi-hibernation until the weather warms to at least 55° F and the sun warms their wings. Then they leave the tree to find water or to mate.

Female monarchs don't lay eggs immediately. They wait until late February to begin the journey north. Then they each lay up to 100 eggs on milkweed plants. The first generation of monarchs that migrated south now dies after living six to nine months. The second and third generations live six weeks each and then die. The fourth returns to Canada and produces the fifth generation, which completes the cycle by migrating south.

How do monarchs know to migrate and know where to go? The information passes from parent to child in a process called intergenerational memory. Along the way some of the North American monarchs must have been blown off course or had a memory lapse. These intrepid fliers have crossed the Atlantic Ocean to live in the Azores and Canary Islands and crossed the Pacific to live in Australia and New Zealand.

COPYCAT COLORS

Sharing similar looks, the toxic viceroy butterfly, above, and poisonous monarch, right, send a double-winged message to predators – beware! Monarchs gather in a streambed to drink moisture and take in minerals and salts. These groups are known as "mud-puddling clubs."

MASTERS OF DISGUISE

BUTTERFLIES AND MOTHS, EVEN THE hardiest long-distance travelers, face continual danger from predators. Vertebrate predators include birds, bats, mice, monkeys, lizards, frogs, fish, and small snakes. Invertebrate enemies are spiders, ants, beetles, dragonflies, scorpions, centipedes, and wasps. North American whitefaced hornets can even catch speedy butterflies like the American copper.

Despite all these hungry creatures waiting for a tasty meal, most butterflies manage to survive. Like caterpillars, they wear disguises. They also deceive predators with nearly flawless impersonations.

The monarch butterfly, which eats toxic milkweed as a caterpillar, retains the poison in its body, especially the wings. After sampling a monarch wing, birds as large as a blue jay become ill, and small lizards can die. Once predators discover the toxicity, they leave monarchs alone.

The bright orange viceroy butterfly closely resembles the monarch. Beginning in the mid-1800s, lepidopterists believed the viceroy was non-poisonous and that by impersonating the monarch it was left alone. Recent studies show the viceroy has over the years developed its own toxic defense. But by continuing to share colors, fewer monarchs and viceroys are sampled before predators learn to avoid them. Aside from these two, hundreds of edible species share color patterns with inedible ones well enough to discourage predators, a condition called mimicry.

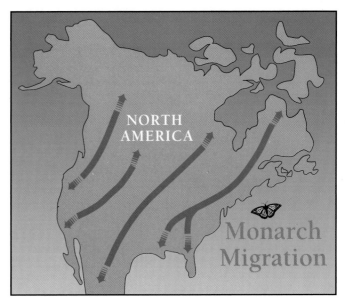

Millions of monarch butterflies travel up to 4,000 miles on their annual migration from Canada into the United States and Mexico.

The distasteful pipevine swallowtail butterfly, found throughout much of the United States, attracts several mimics. Along with duplicate colors, the impersonators copy the pipevine's flight patterns. One imitator, the red-spotted purple butterfly in the south, is related to the white admiral butterfly, a northern species. These two look completely different. Because no pipevine swallowtails live in the north, the white admiral has no example to mimic.

Tasty butterflies that don't mimic toxic ones often have better-developed muscles for flying faster and more erratically to avoid capture. These, in turn, are imitated by butterflies that both taste good and fly slowly.

What about butterflies and moths without poisons or mimic coloring? Some part of them resembles their environment closely enough to blend in. Master of this disguise is the Indian leaf butterfly in southeast Asia. Its orange and blue upper wings attract attention from hungry birds. If it cannot outrun them, it does a disappearing act. The Indian leaf alights on a branch or on the ground in leaf litter. By folding its wings over its back, a butterfly in this species looks just like a dead leaf.

END OF THE LINE

Despite their many defenses, butterflies and caterpillars often fall victim to predators. Enemies include a nursery web spider, left, and a blue-crowned motmot, above. Eggs laid by a wasp become parasites on the caterpillar at right. After hatching, the wasp larvas feed on the body, soon killing it.

Butterflies also use eyespots to confuse their enemies. These patches of color on the back wings look like large eyes. They can startle a bird into leaving or cause it to snatch a butterfly's back wings where it will do less harm. Even with a bite out of the back wing, the insect can fly.

Although most butterflies roost separately, some species sleep in groups for extra protection. Clusters of poisonous butterflies give off strong odors to warn away enemies. Predators only need to sample one insect to know the rest are off-limits. Daggerwing butterflies in Costa Rica cluster together in the same place every night, all facing out. If one is disturbed and spreads its wings, a domino effect ripples through to alert the entire group.

FILL 'ER UP

A BUTTERFLY PERCHES ON A FLOWER. ITS LONG tongue sips nectar from deep within the flower's heart. Feet and head dusted with pollen, the creature flies to another flower to feed and to cross-pollinate. Only bees pollinate better than butterflies and moths.

Often flowers that moths visit have deep necks. Moth's lengthy tongues – from nine to 14 inches for some species in the tropics – are the only way to reach the nectar.

Most species use nectar as their main source of energy. But butterflies and moths also require substances in their diet such as nitrogen and amino acids for protein. Some flowers accommodate them by providing ten to 14 percent amino acids in the nectar. Flowers that attract bees and hummingbirds only have five percent. Other sources of protein include tree sap, juices of rotting fruit, honeydew from aphids and other insects, and animal dung.

Butterflies often crowd around these unusual feeding sources, as well as at puddles of liquid. In addition to sucking dew from leaves, clouds of butterflies congregate at mud puddles, on stream banks, on damp ground after rain, or on urine-soaked ground. They may stay at these watering holes for hours. Lepidopterists believe the males remove minerals and salts from the liquid. Butterflies in the tropics also land on humans to sip salty sweat off skin and clothes.

Some butterflies and moths have adjusted to landscapes altered by humans. Others have not. The xerces blue butterfly disappeared from San Francisco, California, in 1934 when urban development eliminated its habitat. A few species have been able to adapt to living in landfills, unplanted fields, and vacant lots.

WINGWORKS

Red lacewing butterflies in Australia
ready their wings for an inaugural
flight. Muscles inside the thorax
raise and lower the wings.
Smaller muscles control their angle
and position. When a butterfly glides,
the wings flap slowly.
When alarmed, they beat quickly,
and the wing ends almost touch
at top and bottom.

TWILIGHT IN THE TEMPERATE ZONE

*C*overed with dew, the American copper butterfly, right, waits for the sun to warm its wings. Coppers live in temperate climates of warm summers and cold winters, in forests of East Africa and North America, and in mountains of northern Europe and New Zealand. Large coppers disappeared from England, Europe and parts of Asia as their habitats vanished.

ON A WING AND A PRAYER

BUTTERFLIES HAVE LONG HELD A FASCINATION for humans. Ancient Greeks and others saw them as departed souls of the dead. Oriental lore celebrated their free spirit and beauty. During the Middle Ages, caterpillars were thought to be completely unrelated to butterflies. Today butterflies and moths are viewed in several ways. They are appreciated for their complex life cycle. They're studied for their role as indicators of the environment's health. And their populations are recognized as being endangered by development worldwide.

MASS OF MONARCHS

A winter cluster of monarch butterflies, right, sunbathes before flight. Monarchs' winter habitat has been reduced over the years because of development. An annual monarch butterfly parade in Pacific Grove, California, above, celebrates their life.

Destruction of their habitat is the greatest threat to butterflies. Concrete paves over meadows. Grasslands face drought and overgrazing by livestock. Wetlands suffer from drainage and changes in sea level caused by global warming. Tropical rainforests lose thousands of acres daily to lumbering. Insecticides and industrial pollution kill butterflies at every stage of their life cycle.

In most cases, collectors of butterflies and moths don't endanger a species. Collection of dwindling species is now controlled or forbidden by their native countries. Butterflies like the paradise birdwing in Papua New Guinea and homerus swallowtail in Jamaica are scarce, they have slow reproduction rates, and their habitats are declining. Further reducing their numbers for butterfly collections would seriously endanger them.

Efforts to preserve butterfly and moth populations have benefitted by the increase of butterfly farms. Located in countries throughout the world, the farms breed butterflies for collectors, zoos, and butterfly houses. Most farms are set up in undeveloped areas in the tropics, where they provide income for local residents and eduction about conserving native forests.

On a smaller scale, we can help preserve butterflies, moths, and their environments. Our gardens can include plants with nectar and others with leaves for caterpillars. Butterflies favor colorful plants massed together and flat stones placed as a perch to warm their wings. Include a pool of shallow water for them to drink. Avoid pesticides.

The beauty, metamorphosis, and untamed grace of butterflies inspire us to appreciate the natural world. That should never change.

ABOUT THE PHOTOGRAPHERS

Stanley Breeden/DRK Photo: page 9 right, inside back cover

D. Cavagnaro/DRK Photo: page 24 lower photo

Hal Clason: page 29

Michael Fogden/DRK Photo: pages 8, 22-23

Jeff Foott: pages 16, 17 left, 17 right, 19, 36

John Gerlach/DRK Photo: page 28

Richard R. Hansen: front cover, pages 37, 40

Alex Kerstitch: page 27 inset, back cover

Frans Lanting/Minden Pictures: page 18

Robert and Linda Mitchell: inside front cover, pages 5 upper photo, 6, 7, 9 left, 12, 13, 14-15, 20-21, 24 upper photo

Jeanette Sainz: page 10 inset

Kjell B. Sandved/Photo Researchers: page 26 inset

Kevin Schafer and Martha Hill: pages 26-27, 31 upper photo, 31 lower photo

Larry Ulrich/DRK Photo: pages 10-11, 34-35

Larry West: pages 1, 2-3, 23 inset, 30, 35 inset

Belinda Wright/DRK Photo: pages 4, 5 lower photo, 33

ABOUT THE AUTHOR

A Shimmer of Butterflies marks the third book Joni Phelps Hunt has written for Blake Publishing. Her previous titles are *The Desert* and *A Chorus of Frogs.* Joni enjoys watching the world undergo metamorphosis.

SPECIAL THANKS

Julian Burgess, Manager, London Butterfly House
Boyce Drummond, The Lepidopterists' Society
Gary Dunn, Y.E.S. (Young Entomologists' Society)
William D. Winter, The Lepidopterists' Society

TO LEARN MORE

🦋 **The Lepidopterists' Society**, 257 Common Street, Dedham, Massachusetts 02026-4020

🦋 **Xerces Society**, 10 Southwest Ash Street, Portland, Oregon 97204

🦋 **Y.E.S.** (Young Entomologists' Society), 1915 Peggy Place, Lansing, Michigan 48910

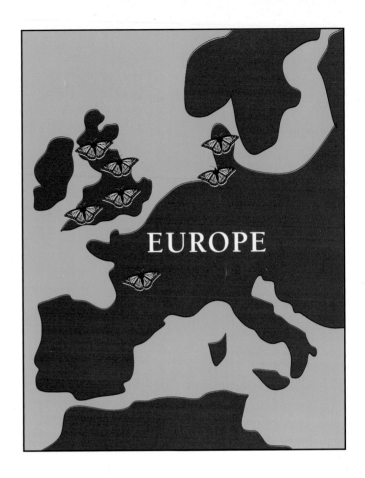

EUROPE

BOOKS

🦋 *Butterfly and Moth,* by Paul Whalley (Knopf, 1988)

🦋 *The Butterfly Book – An Easy Guide to Butterfly Gardening, Identification and Behavior,* by Donald and Lillian Stokes (Little, Brown & Co., 1991)

🦋 *Butterfly Gardening – Creating Summer Magic in Your Garden,* by The Xerces Society and The Smithsonian Institution (Sierra Club Books, 1990)

🦋 *Discover Butterflies!,* The Callaway Foundation (1991)

🦋 *Handbook for Butterfly Watchers,* by Robert Michael Pyle (Houghton-Mifflin, 1992)

FILMS

🦋 Callaway Gardens video (Day Butterfly Center)

🦋 Pretty Insects video (Our Natural Heritage Series)

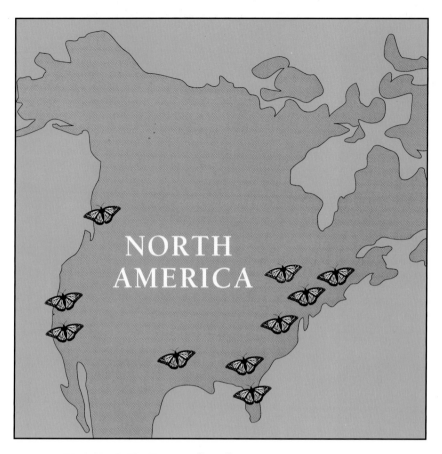

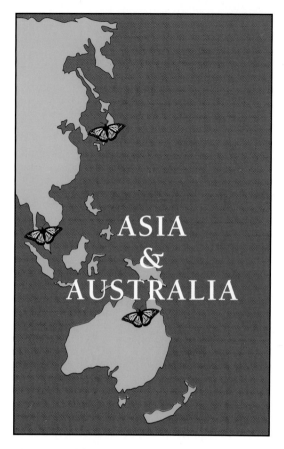

WHERE TO SEE BUTTERFLIES WORLDWIDE

Butterfly parks, gardens, and farms offer opportunities for viewing many species, including those not native to the region. Most places listed charge an admission fee.

EUROPE (a partial list)
Denmark
• *Tropisk Sommerfugle Farm* (Tropical Butterfly Farm)
Loftbrovej 15
DK-9400 Norresundby
France
• *Jardin des Papillons*
63 bis Avenue de Champagne
51200 Epernay
• *La Jungle des Papillons*
309 Avenue Mozart
0600 Antibes
The Netherlands
• *Noorder Dierenpark*
Zoo Emmen
Hoofdstraat 18
Postbus 1010
7801 BA Emmen
• *Insectarium*
Hortus Haren
Kerklaan 34
9751 NN Haren
United Kingdom
•*London Butterfly House*
Syon Park
Brentford, Middlesex
• *New Forest Butterfly Farm*
Longdown
Ashurst, Southampton

• *Edinburgh Butterfly Farm*
Doobies Garden Centre
Edinburgh, Scotland
• *Butterfly Palace* (Pili Palas)
Ffordd Penmynyd, Porthaethwy
Ynys Mon, Gwynedd, Wales
• *Isle of Wight Butterfly World*
Medina Garden Centre, Staplers Road
Wooton, Ryde, Isle of Wight
• *Long Sutton Butterfly Park*
Little London, Long Sutton
Spalding, Lincolnshire
• *The Butterfly House*
Windsor Safaris Park
Winkfield Road
Windsor, Berkshire

NORTH AMERICA (a partial list)
United States
• *Seasonal monarch viewing in California at Santa Cruz, Pacific Grove, Monterey Peninsula, Morro Bay, Pismo Beach, Gaviota, and Santa Barbara*
• *Butterfly World*
Marine World Africa – USA
Marine World Parkway
Vallejo, California 94589
• *Butterfly World*
Tradewinds Park South
3600 W. Sample Road
Coconut Creek, Florida 33073
• *Day Butterfly Center*
Callaway Gardens
Pine Mountain, Georgia 31822

• *The Butterfly Place at Papillon Park*
120 Tyngsboro Road
Westford, Massachusetts 01886
•*Butterfly Aviary and Garden*
Cincinnati Zoo
3400 Vine Street
Cincinnati, Ohio 45220
• *The Butterfly House*
Mercer Arboretum and Botanic Gardens
22306 Aldine Westfield
Humble, Texas 77338
Canada
• *Butterfly World*
P.O. Box 36
Coombs, British Columbia VOR 1MO
• *Butterfly World*
Central Saanich, British Columbia V8X 3X1

ASIA & AUSTRALIA (a partial list)
Australia
• *Australian Butterfly Sanctuary*
P.O. Box 345, Kennedy Highway
Kuranda, Queensland 4872
Japan
•*Nawa Insect Museum*
2 Omiya-Cho
Gifu City
•*Tama Zoo*
300 Hodokubo
Hino City, Tokyo
Malaysia
• *Penang Butterfly Farm*
No. 830, Mk 2
Jalan Teluk Bahang
11050 Penang

Indian cup moth caterpillars at lunch

We think of butterflies as the glamorous ones,
but moths are small miracles
and caterpillars as well,
if we take the time to peer closely.
Come, explore with us
the brilliant career of butterflies & moths.